A BLUE BANNER
BIOGRAPHY

Ashton Kutcher

Jennifer Torres

P.O. Box 196
Hockessin, Delaware 19707
Visit us on the web: www.mitchelllane.com
Comments? email us: mitchelllane@mitchelllane.com

Printing   1   2   3   4   5   6   7   8

Blue Banner Biographies

Alicia Keys	Allen Iverson	Ashanti
Ashlee Simpson	**Ashton Kutcher**	Avril Lavigne
Beyoncé	Bow Wow	Britney Spears
Christina Aguilera	Christopher Paul Curtis	Clay Aiken
Condoleezza Rice	Daniel Radcliffe	Derek Jeter
Eminem	Eve	Ja Rule
Jay-Z	Jennifer Lopez	J. K. Rowling
Jodie Foster	Justin Berfield	Kate Hudson
Lance Armstrong	Lindsay Lohan	Mario
Mary-Kate and Ashley Olsen	Melissa Gilbert	Michael Jackson
Missy Elliott	Nelly	P. Diddy
Paris Hilton	Queen Latifah	Rita Williams-Garcia
Ritchie Valens	Ron Howard	Rudy Giuliani
Sally Field	Selena	Shirley Temple
Usher		

Library of Congress Cataloging-in-Publication Data
Torres, Jennifer.
    Ashton Kutcher / by Jennifer Torres.
        p. cm. — (A blue banner biography)
    Includes bibliographical references and index.
    ISBN 1-58415-380-6 (library bound)
    1. Kutcher, Ashton, 1978—Juvenile literature. 2. Actors—United States—Biography—Juvenile literature. I. Title. II. Series.
PN2287.K88T67 2005
792.02'8'092—dc22
                                                                                                    2004030254

ABOUT THE AUTHOR: Jennifer Torres is a freelance writer and newspaper columnist based in Central Florida. Her articles have appeared in newspapers, parenting journals, and women's magazines across the country and Canada. She has also written books for Mitchell Lane including *Eve, Paris Hilton, Kate Hudson,* and *Ashanti.* When she's not writing she enjoys spending time at the beach with her husband John and their five children, Timothy, Emily, Isabelle, Daniel, and Jacqueline.
PHOTO CREDITS: Cover—Evan Agostini/Getty Images; p. 4—Stephen Shugerman/Getty Images; p. 8—RJ Capak/WireImage; pp. 12, 14—Jon Kopaloff/Getty Images; p. 21—COS via Getty Images; p. 22—Kevin Winter/Getty Images; p. 24—Newsmakers/Getty Images; p. 25—Dave Benett/Getty Images; p. 26—Mark Mainz/Getty Images; p. 28—Giulio Marcocchi/Getty Images.

CONTENTS

Ashton Kutcher came from the farms of Cedar Rapids, Iowa, to the bright lights and big city of Hollywood.

"Punk'd"

*T*he special agent looked very serious.

As he and his team removed jewelry, clothes, and furniture from the huge mansion, singer Justin Timberlake looked on in horror.

After all, this was the young pop star's mansion, and those were his things.

He had no idea why they were being taken away.

The special agent said Timberlake owed $900,000 in taxes. To pay the bill, the government was taking away all his stuff. Timberlake was very upset. He couldn't believe this was happening.

"We'll also be taking your dogs," the agent said.

"My dogs!" Timberlake cried. This was unreal. This couldn't be legal! What was he going to do? His life was destroyed!

Somewhere just out of view, Ashton Kutcher couldn't stop giggling.

The handsome twenty-six-year-old was watching the whole scene on a television screen and enjoying every minute of it.

As Timberlake picked up the phone to call his mother, tears welled in his eyes. That's when Kutcher knew Timberlake had had enough. He left the video booth where he was hidden away and walked toward his victim.

When Timberlake saw Kutcher, his eyes opened wide and he laughed out loud.

He wasn't really in trouble. He had been "punk'd"!

Punk'd is a show Ashton Kutcher helped create. For the show, he tricks stars into thinking something bad is happening to them when it's really not. It is TV's version of an April Fool's Day joke caught on camera.

But not all stars think the pranks are funny.

Timberlake's friend Alyssa Milano, who stars on the hit television show *Charmed*, was angry.

"I knew that they were going to do that to him, and I wanted to call him and ruin it so bad," she said. "They wanted to get me, and someone told me, thank the Lord. They wanted to set up some sort of satellite in my backyard and say they got alien signals."

Punk'd is a show Ashton Kutcher helped create. For the show, he tricks stars into thinking something bad is happening to them when it's really not.

Even though he didn't fool Milano, Kutcher has "punk'd" some of Hollywood's biggest names, including Jessica Simpson, Hilary Duff, Beyonce, Pink, Christina Aguilera, Britney Spears, and Usher.

The show, which first aired on MTV in 2003, has become a big hit. That's why when Kutcher announced he was ending the show after only two seasons, fans were very upset. In magazines and on television, Kutcher told the world that *Punk'd* was over. He said he couldn't think of any new ideas and wanted to work on other projects.

"I get bored really, really quickly and I think that there are other things that we can do," said Kutcher. "You have to remember that the MTV audience is an extremely fickle audience, right, and they like things for this long and then, they find the next cool thing that exists. That's how that place works. So, if you can't change it and make it new and make it different, and make it the new hot thing, don't do it because you're going to fall off the cliff."

But it turns out his fans were "punk'd"!

On April 1, 2004 — April Fool's Day — Kutcher said he was "just kidding" and the show would go on for a third season. It was the most watched season to date. About 3.2 million people watched every time the show aired.

> ... *Kutcher has "punk'd" some of Hollywood's biggest names, including Jessica Simpson, Hilary Duff, Beyonce, ... Britney Spears and Usher.*

While *Punk'd* is a very popular show, many also know Ashton Kutcher as the zany Michael Kelso from *That '70s Show*, a television series that follows the lives of six typical teenagers who are growing up in the 1970s.

In fact, being "zany" is something Kutcher is well known for in Hollywood. In addition to TV, he's had big-screen roles in several wacky comedies. Some of them are *Dude, Where's My Car?*, *My Boss's Daughter*, *Just Married*, *Cheaper by the Dozen*, *Guess Who*, and *A Lot Like Love*.

But Ashton's life wasn't always filled with laughter.

Ashton Kutcher and Amanda Pete had fun together making the comedy film A Lot Like Love.

A Long Way to Hollywood

*O*n February 7, 1978, in the farming town of Cedar Rapids, Iowa, twin boys were born to Larry and Diane Kutcher. The first they named Christopher Ashton Kutcher. He was healthy and active. Moments later, his brother, Michael Kutcher, was born.

Something was wrong.

Michael's cry was softer. He seemed weaker. The doctor told the new parents that Michael had to spend more time in the hospital to find out if he was sick. For three months, baby Michael stayed in an incubator at the hospital. An incubator looks like a baby's crib, but it is kept clean and warm to help the baby grow stronger.

After the baby was at the hospital for a while, doctors found out that Michael had a mild case of cerebral palsy. This is a disease that can affect body movement. It can make it hard for a person to walk or to control the way he or she moves. Some people who have cerebral palsy also have a difficult time talking. There is no cure for it.

Despite Michael's cerebral palsy, the twin boys and their older sister, Tausha, had lots of fun together. Growing up, they were all very close. They had to be! In their rural town, the closest neighbors were miles away.

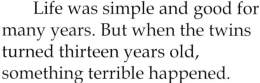

> **Despite Michael's cerebral palsy, the twin boys and their older sister, Tausha, had lots of fun together. Growing up, they were all very close.**

Life was simple and good for many years. But when the twins turned thirteen years old, something terrible happened.

Michael became gravely ill. He suffered from cardiomyopathy (KAR-dee-oh-my-AH-pah-thee). It is a disease of the heart muscle. When someone suffers from cardiomyopathy, his or her heart muscle becomes swollen and doesn't work as well as it should.

The day it happened to Michael had started off normally. Suddenly Michael had trouble breathing. He became dizzy, and soon he had very bad chest pains. His mom and dad rushed him to the hospital. Christopher and Tausha were very worried about their brother.

And the news was bad.

To survive, Michael would need a heart transplant. His own heart was no longer working the right way. He would need to have his heart taken out and a healthy heart put in its place. A new heart that would work in Michael's body would be hard to find.

"We didn't know if Mike would survive," said Rita, his aunt. "Chris was very young but he led the whole family with a prayer he made up on the spot."

The Kutcher family stayed by Michael's bed for two days. Finally some wonderful news arrived. A heart had been found!

Michael was wheeled into the operating room. Four hours later he had a new, healthy heart in his body.

His family was very happy.

The next day Christopher, who would become known by his middle name of Ashton, went to school and warned the other kids that they had better not tease Michael when he came back to class. He wasn't about to let anyone hurt his brother's feelings. Ever.

When Michael finally came home, Ashton made his brother feel relaxed by joking with him about the operation.

"At some level, Ashton's joking around was a way of lightening the mood with his brother Michael," said childhood friend Joy Janda.

When Michael finally came home, Ashton made his brother feel relaxed by joking with him about the operation.

"Chris treated Mike as an equal even though he was not as mature in many ways," said an old friend named Erin Cervantes. "Mike was self-conscious about his health. He was weaker and slower but Chris always made sure he was treated just the same."

Ashton spends a lot of time with his mom, Diane, because family is a priority in his life.

Changes

*A*shton was very happy that his brother was going to be all right. He thought of Michael as his hero, because even though he had to suffer through so much, he was still very strong and a very good person. It was at that moment Ashton knew he wanted to help find a cure for cerebral palsy.

Before he could think about that too much, some more bad news came.

His father, who worked as a butcher, lost his job.

But far worse news came next. His parents were getting a divorce.

Life was changing very fast. Within two years Ashton's mom remarried a construction worker named Mark Portwood. The whole family moved to Homestead, Iowa. Ashton thought his hometown was small, but it was huge compared to Homestead. Barely 100 people lived in the small farming community.

Even though Ashton's parents divorced when he was a young boy, his father Larry remains very involved in his life.

"It was pretty much one of those communities where we all had to make our own entertainment, so I did a lot of hunting and shooting and fishing, all things that come naturally in the countryside," said Kutcher. "And I was heavily into the Boy Scouts. . . . Oh, and school drama stuff—plays and such . . . in an environment like that, you get very creative when it comes to having fun."

To make friends, Ashton got involved in sports like wrestling. He did very well. But what really made him happy was being on stage. Even though his new high school was small, it had a nice theater where students could perform plays. Ashton still had dreams of curing his brother, but the more he acted in plays, the more he loved it. When a teacher at his school told him he was really good at it, Ashton was inspired. "I'll always thank him for that. Mr. Cervantes is his name. He actually told me I was good," said Kutcher. "I think it was the first time someone told me I was good at something. That I was talented and good."

Ashton tried out for several plays and won small parts in many of them. Finally he got a big role in the musical *Annie*. *Annie* is the story of a young orphan who is taken in by a rich man named Daddy Warbucks. Daddy Warbucks was a very important

> *To make friends, Ashton got involved in sports like wrestling. He did very well. But what really made him happy was being on stage.*

character, and Ashton was to play him. He was happy and excited. Acting was something he loved. He even began to think about doing it as a career after school.

Then a bad decision changed everything.

> **Sometimes when kids want to fit in, they do foolish things. Ashton did a few very foolish things.**

Sometimes when kids want to fit in, they do foolish things. Ashton did a very few very foolish things. First he brought beer to a school function. Then he tried to steal money from a school soda machine.

Not only did Ashton lose his role in the school play, but he was also sent to jail for the night. His mother and stepfather were not pleased.

"I broke into my high school when I was a senior and was thrown in jail. My friends and I were going to steal money out of the soda machine. My stepdad told me if I ever got thrown in jail, he would let me stay there for the night," said Kutcher. "I called him and said, 'Hey, I'm in jail.' And he's like, 'Have a good night' and hung up the phone!"

A night in jail wasn't the only result of his bad choices. Ashton was charged with breaking and entering. He had to spend three years on probation (proe-BAY-shun). Probation meant he wouldn't have to go back to jail. Instead, he had to check in with a probation officer. The officer made sure Ashton was following all the rules. If Ashton broke any rule at all, he would have to spend the rest of the three years in jail. On probation, he was not allowed to move very far from home.

After graduating from high school, Ashton had to put his dream of being an actor on hold. There weren't many acting jobs in Iowa. Ashton would have a better chance of finding work in New York — a place he couldn't go while on probation.

Acting wasn't the only dream he had. Ashton wanted to find a cure for cerebral palsy, the disease that affected his brother. To do that, he went to the University of Iowa and studied biochemical engineering. This is the study of how and why the body acts in certain ways. Ashton hoped he could use his education to help his brother.

School was expensive, so Ashton made some money doing a few odd jobs. He swept up cereal that had fallen on the floor at a cereal factory. He skinned deer. He washed a lot of dishes. Ashton also found out he could make money by giving some of his blood to a hospital, so he did that too.

Once again, life had a surprise in store for Ashton. This time though, the news was good.

> *Acting wasn't the only dream he had. Ashton wanted to find a cure for cerebral palsy, the disease that affected his brother.*

Discovered

After he'd had enough of cereal sweeping and deer skinning, Ashton got a job as a waiter. One day someone came in who changed his life. It was a local modeling agent. The agent told Ashton he should enter a modeling contest.

The contest was called *The Fresh Faces of Iowa*.

Ashton entered and won.

The prize was a trip to New York City. There he would compete in the International Model and Talent Agency Competition. He didn't win the contest, but he was signed with a modeling agency. The agency thought Ashton's good looks could take him to the top of the modeling world.

Pretty soon this small-town boy was traveling the world. As a model, Ashton wore clothes created by top designers like Versace, Tommy Hilfiger, and Calvin Klein. He wore the clothes in fashion shows in front of crowds of people. Ashton's picture also appeared on magazine covers and billboards. He became a top model. Everyone wanted him to wear their clothes. When Ashton wore them, the company sold a lot of clothes.

Even though Ashton was happy to get noticed, he secretly wished he could be an actor instead of a model. Modeling seemed a bit "silly" to him.

"It's a very silly way of earning a living," said Kutcher. "It's the least important job in the world, isn't it? Just being a coat hanger for other people's frocks and creations. And boy, there were some weird and wacky things that we were expected and required to wear, things that were just totally embarrassing."

Before he was an actor, Ashton worked as a top model for designers like Tommy Hilfiger and Calvin Klein. He thought it was silly, but it was one step in the right direction for his acting career.

He had to admit that modeling wasn't all bad. There were some really wonderful things about being a model.

"The great thing was, and I am very grateful for this, there was a lot of traveling and I got to see some great places, Milan, Rome, London, a lot of the rest of Europe," said Kutcher. "And I appreciated that, I was being paid to do something that I would never otherwise have done. I loved coming over [to England] for the first time, seeing all the history."

But Ashton still wanted to try acting. With the help of his agent, he started looking for acting roles. He traveled to Los Angeles, California, where he got his first big break.

"I'd gone down to NBC Studios and I was in to read for something or other, and it didn't go very well," said Kutcher. "I was in the lobby, on my way out, and this other guy came up to me, clapped me on the back, and asked if I wouldn't mind reading for another script with him."

Ashton said yes and followed the man back to his office. He read some lines from the script.

He soon realized the story was about a cowboy surfer in Hawaii. This sounded silly to Ashton. However, he read the lines really well and the man liked him a lot. He might have

> *He had to admit that modeling wasn't all that bad. There were some really wonderful things about being a model. . . . But Ashton still wanted to try acting.*

even given Ashton the role, but Ashton had to leave for another appointment.

"My next appointment [was] over at Fox TV, for a read-through of what became That Seventies Show," said Kutcher. "And I loved it, the idea was cool and the people were great and they offered me the role on the spot."

At that moment, Ashton's phone rang.

"It was the people at NBC offering me the part in their project! And when I politely declined it, they weren't very happy!" said Kutcher.

It was, after all, their loss. In 1998 *That '70s Show* became a hit. It was only the beginning for Ashton.

Ashton stands with other cast members of the hit television show That 70's Show *during the Church of Scientology's 11th Annual Christmas Stories Fundraisers. From left to right: Wilmer Valderrama, Laura Prepon, Mila Kunis, Ashton Kutcher, and Danny Masterson.*

Ashton was honored for his sense of fashion style at the VH1 Big in 2003 Awards.

Success

That '70s Show is about teenagers growing up in the Wisconsin suburbs in the 1970s. The public loved it! In the show, Ashton plays the role of Michael Kelso.

Because the show was so popular, Ashton became popular too. He began to get offers to appear in movies. Ashton landed some small roles. He played in *Coming Soon* in 1999, and in the films *Down to You* and *Reindeer Games* in 2000. But he really got a chance to shine when he won a starring role in the 2000 comedy *Dude, Where's My Car?* The movie is about two guys trying to find their lost car. It is a pretty simple plot, but many people seem to enjoy the movie.

For his part, Ashton was nominated for an award. It was for Best Male Newcomer at Las Vegas Film Critics Society Awards.

Ashton says he owes much of his talent in comedy to a writer he met long ago. The writer had told him the secret of comedy. The secret is, "You don't try to be funny."

In 2000, Ashton, here with fellow cast members, got the starring role in the comedy movie Dude Where's My Car? *From left to right: Marla Sokoloff, Seann William Scott, Ashton Kutcher, and Jennifer Garner.*

It must be working. *That '70s Show* has been on television for more than seven seasons. Ashton decided not to renew his contract for an eighth season. He wanted to continue to star in more movies.

In 2003 he filmed *My Boss's Daughter*. Then he was in the comedy *Just Married*. That same year he starred in another comedy called *Cheaper by the Dozen*. This movie is about a family that has twelve kids!

Well known for his comedy, Ashton decided it was time for a change.

In 2004, Ashton starred in a drama called *The Butterfly Effect*. He played the role of Evan Treborn, a young man with severe memory problems. The movie got its name from something called the chaos theory. It is not an easy theory to explain. Simply put, it asks the question, "If a butterfly flaps its wings on one side of the world, does it cause a wind storm on the other side?" In other words, does everything we do affect everything else? Ashton was excited about the plot. His fans came out in force to see it. *The Butterfly Effect* showed the world that Ashton could be more than just "funny."

In 2003 Ashton co-starred in the movie Just Married *with then girlfriend Brittany Murphy.*

Ashton plays the role of Evan Treborn in the movie The Butterfly Effect.

These days Ashton is very busy. He's still working on *Punk'd*. He also has several new movies coming out. One is an animated movie called *Open Season*. It is about a deer and a grizzly bear stuck in the forest during hunting season. Ashton is also making news because his current girlfriend is the well-known actress Demi Moore. She is much older than Ashton, so some people wonder if their relationship will last. But both seem very happy.

As for his brother, Ashton and he remain very close. He visits Michael at his home in Iowa often and says his brother is living a happy life.

Ashton continues to be very thankful to the doctors and nurses at the University of Iowa Hospitals in Iowa City, where his brother was treated as a young boy. Fox, the network that produces *That '70s Show*, gave $32,000 to the hospitals' Patient Transplant Support Fund, and Kutcher makes regular donations to the fund as well.

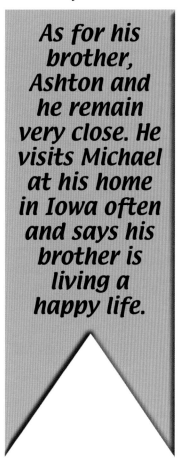

As for his brother, Ashton and he remain very close. He visits Michael at his home in Iowa often and says his brother is living a happy life.

Whatever else the future holds, Ashton is ready.

Stars don't always come from the brightest beginnings.

Ashton grew up in a small town. Like many other kids, his parents divorced. His brother suffered a life-threatening disease. Ashton made mistakes along the way. Now he is a star.

"I think these are the obstacles that are in our way that we are to overcome as people," said Kutcher. "That's really what we are here for, to overcome our obstacles."

After years of searching for his place in life, Ashton learned he was always exactly where he needed to be.

"I started to believe in myself a little bit more. If I really wanted something I could have it, anything was possible," said Kutcher. "I grew up a lot and I've realized the responsibility that I have as a person and that my actions count and I can make a difference with my actions."

And so, he says, can everybody else.

Ashton is now happily involved with actress Demi Moore and is a close friend to her three daughters Rumer (left), Scout (front), and Tallulah Belle (right).

CHRONOLOGY

1978   Christopher Ashton Kutcher is born on February 7 in Cedar Rapids, Iowa, to Larry and Diane Kutcher. His twin brother, Michael, follows; he is born with cerebral palsy.

1991   Michael becomes seriously ill; he gets a heart transplant. Larry Kutcher loses his job of twenty years as a butcher; he and Diane divorce soon after.

1993   Ashton and his family move to tiny Homestead, Iowa.

1995   Ashton breaks into his high school and gets caught. He is put on probation.

1996   Ashton enrolls at the University of Iowa, determined to find a cure for his brother's disease.

1997   Ashton wins *The Fresh Faces of Iowa* modeling contest.

1998   After success as a model, he turns his eye toward acting and lands a role in *That '70s Show.*

2000   He receives praise for his role in the movie *Dude, Where's My Car?*

2003   Ashton begins producing *Punk'd* for MTV. The series becomes a hit.

2004   After a string of comedies, Ashton stars in the drama *The Butterfly Effect.*

2005   Ashton stars in the big-screen movies *Guess Who* and *A Lot Like Love.* He leaves *That 70s Show.* He helps produce the reality show *Beauty and the Geek.* Due to star in the movie *The Guardian* with Kevin Costner.

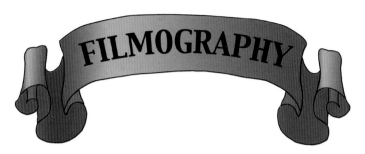

FILMOGRAPHY

The Guardian (2006?)
Open Season (2006)
The Regulators (2005)
A Lot Like Love (2005)
Guess Who (2005)
The Butterfly Effect (2004)
Cheaper by the Dozen (2003)

Just Married (2003)
My Boss's Daughter (2003)
Texas Rangers (2001)
Dude, Where's My Car? (2000)
Reindeer Games (2000)
Down to You (2000)
Coming Soon (1999)

FOR FURTHER READING

Tanith Carey, "Amazing Secrets." Mirror.co.uk, July 2003
http://www.mirror.co.uk/news/allnews/
content_objectid=13144866_method=full_siteid=50143_
headline=-Demi-s-toyboy-was-a-good-kisser----so-gentle-
and-sweet-with-lovely-eyes-name_page.html

Daniel Robert Epstein, "The Butterfly Effect," Underground
Online, January 2004
http://www.allmovieportal.com/m/2003_The_
Butterfly_Effect_ashton_kutcher_interview_bydaniel_
robert_epstein_(ugo_contributing_editor).html

Kate O'Hare, "Doherty and Milano don't care to be Punk'd,"
October 2003
http://tv.zap2it.com/tveditorial/tve_main/
1,1002,271%7C84328%7C1%7C,00.html

Lesley O'Toole, "Ashton Kutcher; The Butterfly Effect," Solis,
2004
http://store.soliscompany.com/askubuef.html

Ashton Kutcher Network, Buzz Archive
http://www.ashton-kutcher.net/

Ashton Kutcher: Drive, VH1
http://www.vh1.com/shows/dyn/driven/76830/
episode.jhtml

INDEX